ABOU
POLZEATH

Michael Williams

BOSSINEY BOOKS

Published by Bossiney Books, St Teath, Bodmin, Cornwall

Typeset and printed by Penwell Ltd, Callington, Cornwall

© Michael Williams

ISBN 0948158 84 0

ACKNOWLEDGEMENTS:

Front cover photography: ROY WESTLAKE
Front cover design: MAGGIE GINGER
Back cover photography: RAY BISHOP
Other photographs: RAY BISHOP, BARRY ENGLEFIELD

At the sea-down's edge between windward and lee …

A.C. Swinburne 1837-1909

About the Author

MICHAEL WILLIAMS, a Cornishman, started full-time publishing in 1975. He and his wife Sonia live in a cottage on the shoulder of a green valley just outside St Teath in North Cornwall.

In addition to writing and publishing, Michael Williams is a keen cricketer and collector of cricket books and autographs. He was the first captain of the Cornish Cricket Club and is today President of the Crusaders. He is also a member of Cornwall and Gloucestershire County Cricket Clubs.

A member of the RSPCA and the International League for the Protection of Horses, he has worked hard for reform in laws relating to animal welfare. Locally, he is a patron of the Broomfield Horse Sanctuary near Penzance.

His latest contribution to the Bossiney list is as co-author with Felicity Young of King Arthur in the West. *Other recent Cornish titles include* Curious Cornwall *and* Strange Stories of Cornwall. *As a publisher he now operates in six regions: Cornwall, Devon, Dorset, Somerset, Avon and Wiltshire. Here, in words and pictures, he explores Polzeath.*

Polzeath – and Tourism

THE coming of the railways to Cornwall coincided with the real development of tourism west of the Tamar – the London and SouthWestern running a line into North Cornwall via Okehampton.

Here is how an early travel writer saw things in a guide called *The North Cornwall Coast:*

'From St. Enodoc we find the field path through Trebetherick village, the houses standing beyond the church, to Polzeath. At the top of the hill is the coastguard station, and a building containing the life-saving apparatus. We keep to the right, and soon come to the delightful little hamlet of Polzeath. It is a tiny place, with a few houses on the hillside going down to the sea. One of them we shall remember was the residence of "Uncle Zachie", the bird stuffer, and we may wonder which it was, for Polzeath does not offer much choice of dwellings. Polzeath is delightful, with its broad sandy beach, safest for bathing when the tide is rising, and the broad stretch of firm sand above it, through which a little stream runs down from the surrounding hills, spanned by a rustic bridge, so small and fragile-looking that we wonder it is spared by the winter storms. Beyond are the rocky islands of Newland and Gulland, and out into the sea stretches the long black point of Pentire.'

I do not have a publication date for this guide, but guest-house weekly terms range from 25 shillings to 35 shillings. In a section entitled 'Where to stay at Polzeath' the Craig-Var advertised these qualities: 'Furnished Detached House, 7 bedrooms, 9 beds, all with views (uninterrupted) of Sea and Bays; Drawing and Dining Rooms; Bath (h & c), Good Water and Drainage. Apply for particulars to Mrs Craig of Wadebridge.'

We can therefore reasonably assume it was not long after 1908, the date of the first edition. In her introduction Beatrix Cresswell wrote 'Out of England, into Cornwall the force of this saying becomes speedily apparent to any one who crosses the Tamar and enters the Duchy … The churches and villages bear names that many of us have never heard before; the names of the old British saints.'

These were the days when a coach and four would meet the trains to and from Waterloo. The train journey from Waterloo to Wadebridge was a matter of 254 ¼ miles and the cheapest return fare was 20 shillings and 10 pence.

Through tourism the very character of North Cornwall began to change:

'Art and Book Shop' says the notice. This was the original Stott family shop at the top of the beach. The picture was taken in 1930, almost certainly after a storm. Brian Stott, looking at this photograph in 1993, says it would have been taken after high tide.

cottages offering bed and breakfast, farmers' wives providing Cornish teas, and fishermen rowing the visitors out from the coast to catch fish they would have otherwise caught for themselves.

I recently came across another guide to North Cornwall, this one published nearly thirty years ago. Polzeath earned no more than eleven lines. There is, of course, always a problem of space in any form of publishing, but the fact is Polzeath has become a major tourist area in Cornwall, and tourism is an important plank in the Cornish economy.

The beach at Polzeath – Hayle Bay by name, Hell Bay on some old maps! – is probably the most spacious and popular family beach between Bude and

Polzeath Post Office in 1920 – now the Galleon Cafe. Another picture taken at high tide.

Newquay. Pentireglaze Haven, a sandy inlet, is a continuation of it on the northern side. On either side are impressive cliffs. The beach itself has firm clean sand. Here bathers of all ages can enjoy themselves – bathing is safe and for families there is an important bonus: children are able to play and paddle in safety. Though it's fair to say there is no such thing as a totally safe beach. Bathing may be fun but the sea can be dangerous, especially on those deceptive days when it looks blue and placid. Polzeath is also a splendid surfing rendezvous. Despite the steady stream of development over the years, Polzeath remains a superlative setting at the edge of the Atlantic Ocean.

Stylish surfing …

Surfing

SURFING and Polzeath go together naturally – like strawberries and Cornish cream.

Surf, to the surfer, is the capital L in Life.

Perceptively, accurately, one painter has portrayed surf in the form of white horses, for it literally kicks and bucks and rears.

Well-known local surfer Howard Stott says 'We have this nice wide estuary and these strong waves. Also there's easy access; you have places which are difficult to get to …'

Surfing really took off hereabouts in the 1970s. 'There was some opposition initially,' recalls Howard, 'but now it's accepted as part of the North Cornwall scene. Surfing is now very popular among the schools.' In 1992 the life saving club was started, and Howard Stott is general secretary of Surf to Save, Polzeath's cleaner oceans campaign. He's also vice-chairman of Surfers against Sewage. 'So Polzeath is doing its bit for the UK's environmental surfing. We want clean beaches and clean oceans.'

Surf to Save competitions are held here each September, and inter-schools contests take place at Polzeath in the spring.

Of surfing's appeal he says: 'You have this good mixture of relaxation and excitement. It's a sport with a difference.'

The sea must inevitably feature strongly in a book called *About Polzeath*. Kirsty Gardiner is a young Cornish writer who lives at Lower Trevilla, Feock near Truro. Here is her response to the restless sea, especially written for this publication.

In Celebration

How can I celebrate your splendour, sea?
Your tide that breaks like over-ripe excitement,
No dissolution, indecision in your flow,
Such cold and curious enlightenment,

What of the rocks you thunder over,
They cower beneath the clinging, suffocating sand,
Worn by waves, advancing, reaching out to touch me,
Water's vital, strong, demanding hand,
And the power, heady, overwhelming,
Breaks in never-ending rhythm at my feet,
A ceaseless melody of strength and passion,
Played to nature's wild and fearsome beat,

Here confusion, fear and thunder,
In the crushing, senseless, rushing sea,
Thrown in all directions quick and furious,
Kneel to all the power that can be,

Yet here is beauty and serenity,
The gentle breeze to smooth the water's flow,
Here is peace, with warm and cold entrancement,
Flying high and sweeping deep and low,

Two personalities, with many, varied facets,
Can I ever tire of celebrating and respecting this,
The sea, the purity, the mystery, the ice and fire,
Nature's punishment and nature's glorious kiss.

Kirsty Gardiner

Sir John Betjeman

THERE is great creativity here in Cornwall. Painters and potters, sculptors and writers of all sorts have been inspired by the spirit of ancient Kernow.

Much has been written and created here – probably more than anywhere outside London.

Why?

The question is inevitable, yet unanswerable. But one thing is certain.

This corner of North Cornwall will forever be John Betjeman Country.

Sir John Betjeman was more than the most famous Poet Laureate of all time. In cricketing language, he was an all-rounder: architectural critic, social historian, conservationist writer, railway enthusiast, countryman, humorist, churchman and eccentric. He was all these and a good deal more.

They called him the People's Poet, but as Kenneth Young wrote in his obituary in the *Sunday Telegraph:* '*He was delighted to become Poet Laureate, though he was no snob; he just preferred dining with Dukes than dustmen ...*'

John Betjeman was that very rare bird: a poet and a bestseller. His collected poems, first published way back in 1958, have sold hundreds of thousands of copies and, of course, his popular television appearances were wonderful boosts for publicity. The Cornish vicar, the Reverend Anthony Gent, at his funeral service probably got to the heart of the matter when he said: 'He brought modern poetry from the esoteric to a level where it could be read with enjoyment by the less highbrow and by untold numbers across the world.'

Back in 1975 Sir John generously contributed a chapter to an early Bossiney title *Both Sides of Tamar*, now long out of print:

'*Trebetherick ... it may have been a suburb by the sea and for all our crabbing, fishing and bathing, nothing to do with the real Cornish who regarded us as the foreigners we still are. But for me it was home for the eyes, the nose and the ears. The great, black half-moon of Bray Hill with its three cairns on the top, the long low stretch from Padstow to Stepper Point on the other side of the estuary. The regular cragginess of Newland's rocky island. The changing vegetation of the high-hedged lane ... all these for the eyes. For the nose there was the scent of seaweed and salty sand. Wild mint at one season, honeysuckle and thyme at another; and drying cow-dung*

The former Poet Laureate Sir John Betjeman

always. For the ear there was the roar on the shore when the tide was high. The utter silence when it was low. The larks and oyster-catchers shrill and small, and sea-gulls wailing like angry babies. The rumble of the London and South Western as it crossed the viaduct on its way to the Padstow terminus, the end of that long slow journey of the ambitiously named Atlantic Coast Express.

'This was my Trebetherick.

'Its people are mostly elsewhere. Some in St Enodoc churchyard.'

He loved our wide Cornish skies, the beaches and the changing sea, the cliffs and the churches, and, above all, treasured his boyhood memories of a vanished Cornish way of life. He fell in love with Cornwall as a child, and it was a love affair that never ended, for though he wrote movingly of other places in Britain, Cornwall called him again and again, firing his writing – like a first love that would not let go. Curiously, in the last fortnight of his life, John Murray, his publisher, produced *Betjeman's Cornwall*, a mixture of his poems and prose married to pictures, ancient and modern, and some specially-commissioned drawings by his old friend and collaborator, John Piper. It is a beautiful, evocative celebration.

Cornwall had this tremendous influence on his life: childhood on the sands at Trebetherick, and later golf on this lovely St Enodoc course, Sunday services at St Enodoc Church, a tiny building once buried in sand, and visits to Port Isaac or Padstow across the estuary by ferry, walks on the cliffs, trips inland to beautiful churches like Blisland and Altarnun, tea or a drink with adult friends he had once known as children. Then in the sixties, he acquired a house at Trebetherick called Treen, almost next to the house his father owned when he was a boy.

He died peacefully in his sleep at eight o'clock on Saturday morning May 19 1984 at Trebetherick.

The knight who loved St Pancras Station and trains and disliked Slough – he invoked German bombers 'to mess up the mess they call a town' – had been nursed through a long illness by Lady Elizabeth Cavendish who had been his constant companion for many years.

A frail figure in his last years; Parkinson's disease had confined him to a wheelchair when travelling, enabling him as he once put it 'to play the aged invalid to perfection!' He had a stroke in 1981 and a heart attack in 1983, rallying amazingly, he claimed through the healing qualities of his child-

'The great black half-moon of Bray Hill with its three cairns on the top' as Sir John Betjeman once described this beautiful shape alongside the Camel.

hood teddy-bear Archibald Ormsby-Gore who was rushed to his hospital bedside.

On Tuesday May 22 Sir John Betjeman was buried at his beloved St Enodoc, with its leaning spire, alongside the graves of unknown sailors whose ships had perished on the Doom Bar in the Camel Estuary. It was a simple service – strictly private at the request of his family – the tiny church decorated with wild flowers; oil lamps and candles providing the only light. They carried his coffin between the sand dunes in driving rain, almost gale force conditions – the kind of weather that might have triggered another poem.

St Enodoc Church

ST ENODOC Church is in a truly sporting location: situated on the golf course which also bears its name.

Standing by the churchyard, facing the western face of the Atlantic Ocean, it is difficult to understand that once upon a time the lovely open sea over Daymer Bay was a forest with roaming wild animals. In the year 1857 a thunderous gale, coming off the Atlantic, moved the sands to such a degree stumps and roots of trees and teeth and horns of animals were exposed. But before long the sands covered them again – and today we only have our imagination.

St Enodoc, its little spire pointing like a crooked finger in the direction of heaven, began life seven centuries ago. The little building has suffered cruelly at the hands of the thing we call nature. Early in the nineteenth century the adjoining commons were nothing more than shifting sands and the church was so buried at one stage that in order to maintain the tithes the vicar and his faithful clerk were lowered through a skylight for the only service of the year!

The restoration of St Enodoc took place during 1863-64 and an interesting first-hand account dated 1919-21 was passed to the then vicar. It was in the handwriting of Mr Hart Smith Pearce, the son of the vicar, the Rev Hart Smith, who was responsible for restoring the chapel '... *the sand had blown higher than the eastern gable, the wet came in freely, the high pews were mouldy-green and worm-eaten and bats flew about, living in the belfry. The communion table had two short legs because the rock projected at the foot of the east wall. In 1864 the building was restored, the walls partly rebuilt and on good foundations, the sand removed and the little churchyard cleared and fenced with a good wall, and the roof renewed and new seats provided. It all cost about £550 and I remember the pains and energy my father spent to raise the money ... These works were done by the masons and the workmen of the parish ... with loving care and nothing was destroyed needlessly or removed if it was of use or interest.'*

Furthermore, from the same hand-written account came an unusual story of the chalice: '*When my father was first inducted in 1851 he saw in one of the farmhouses a beautiful Elizabethan chalice, and he felt certain it belonged to St Enodoc. He could never obtain possession but was put off*

16

A rarity: a church on a golf course – St Enodoc.

St Enodoc Church: one of the glories of North Cornwall.

18

with promises, and, of course, he could not prove his suspicions. He kept his eye on it year after year. After he left in 1871 he still kept the chalice under observation, until a new generation came. Visitors appeared frequently and the value of the plate being often discussed, all old pledges were forgotten and a stranger was allowed to purchase it. My father traced him but was again baffled. Finally he heard the chalice was to be sold at Christie's and by shrewd diplomacy and enlisting the sympathy of the firm and other friends, he secured it for £13.10 and restored it after fifty years to the St Enodoc chapel. No doubt the farmer or his parents had originally, as churchwardens, had charge of the plate, and being seldom used, thought it ornamental on the kitchen shelf.'

Sir John Betjeman's final resting place in the churchyard of his beloved St Enodoc.

A Supernatural Postscript

A QUARTER of a century ago, a well-known Cornish painter told me how, one afternoon, she had gone for a walk in North Cornwall, and had come across an old church buried in the sands. Her recollection of the experience was so detailed that she sent me a written account of the strange events of that afternoon – reading her report suggested she had encountered St Enodoc Church in the early 1800s. When I told her so, she confirmed two friends, who had heard her verbal recollection and later read her writing on the subject, said immediately: 'That would have been St Enodoc as it was!'

I was, at the time, researching material for my first supernatural book. Though she had been happy to talk about the incident at length, and to write in detail, the painter refused me permission to publish her story. She did not want the publicity, maybe even feared ridicule. Twenty-five years ago, there was a great deal of cynicism – much of it cruel – on the subject of paranormal possibility. Anyway, though the lady in question has passed on to the great studio in the sky, I continue to respect her confidence – and merely give the outline.

Did she genuinely travel back in time? Or was it a kind of dream – some form of sleep walking perhaps?

Now we shall never know.

OLD POLSEATH AND BEACH

The ribbed face of the sand at Daymer Bay, caught by Barry Englefield's camera on a fine October morning. Bray Hill to the left and Padstow away in the distance.

◀ *A 1910 photograph of old Polseath – spelt with s (as it once was) and not the more recent z.*

21

St Enodoc Golf Club

ONE of the great sporting assets of Cornwall is the St Enodoc Golf Club which boasts one of the finest courses in the Westcountry.

Golfing expert Bernard Darwin described the game here as *'eminently natural, amusing and dramatic in a country of glorious and terrific sand-hills … However I must not talk of the hills too much … there is plenty of fine, open rolling golf country, and it is a feature of many of the holes that the shot has not merely to be hit into the air but hit into the strategic place for the playing of the second. The golf is emphatically in the grand manner.'*

Genesis of both the club and the course is said to be due to a group of undergraduates who in 1888 started playing on the turf around St Enodoc Church and by Daymer Bay; and the official creation of a club is believed to have been in 1891. But it was not until 1907 that the great golfer James Braid – victor of many tournaments – laid out a full 18-hole course which was altered in part in the early 1920s.

The tenancy, originally granted by Dr Hoskin in 1905, was renewed until 1949 when the Duchy of Cornwall, through the secretary Sir Clive Burn, took over all the land and accepted the club as tenants under a lease. Then in 1988 the club purchased the clubhouse, courses and land from the Duchy.

The main course is of championship standard; a nine-hole course was opened in 1967 and later extended to eighteen holes. They share the magnificent views over the estuary and farmland, but the shorter course is more suitable for the beginner and high handicapper. The main course has not changed since Bernard Darwin wrote his splendid piece nearly half a century ago. Recently the length of the course has been extended to 6207 yards: the result of the steady improvement in the tee positions.

Not least for the non-golfers, there is a very pleasant walk over the soft, springy turf, your route being guided by discreetly placed white stones.

St Enodoc has had its royal connections. Back in 1921 – the year that Southern Ireland became the Irish Free State of Eire – the Prince of Wales, the late Duke of Windsor, came to lunch at the club house, after which he accepted the Presidency of St Enodoc, a position he retained until succeeding to the throne. More recently, in 1950, there was a visit by their majesties King George VI and Queen Elizabeth who, with their daughter Princess Margaret, took tea with the club captain and the committee, and even more

Walking by the edge of the ocean at Polzeath.

recently in October 1979, HRH Prince Charles honoured the club by taking
lunch with the captain and officers of St Enodoc.

St Moritz Hotel

THERE has been a hotel here since the 1930s. The St Moritz Hotel stands in a superb position at the mouth of the Camel estuary, set in spacious grounds in an area of outstanding natural beauty. It offers a whole range of facilities: a leisure complex which includes an indoor pool with adjoining children's pool, sauna, steam room, large jacuzzi and snooker table. There is also a room where children can play pool and table tennis. Outdoor activities like horse riding and tennis can be arranged locally by the hotel.

In recent years the owners have built the St Moritz Garden Villas – all beautifully furnished and equipped for comfort.

Inside the hotel Sir John Betjeman is remembered with the Laureate's restaurant where the blend of English and Continental cooking is enhanced by the wide use of fresh North Cornwall produce.

Polzeath from Minver Hill: a postcard dispatched on the seventh day of May 1938.

723   Polzeath from Miniver Hill.

A CORNISH WELCOME

You can 'ave what you like to
ate my dears, you'm very wel-
come to what we've got. · · · ·
There es :—
    Mar'nated Pelch'rds.....
    Cornish Pasty...............
    Hogs' Pudden...............
    Tatie Cake..................
    Figgy 'Obben...............
    Saffern Cake...............
    Bread and Crame.......
    And a nice Dish-o' Tay weth et.

*Food featured on a number of Edwardian picture postcards from Cornwall.
Cards such as this have now become collectors' items. Only about 10 per
cent of those originally published have survived.*

Ken Duxbury, who founded a highly successful sailing school in North Cornwall. A man of varying talents: author, journalist, painter and, most important of all, sailor.

The Coastline

KEN DUXBURY of St Breward is a painter and writer but, above all, he is a sailor, a wise man of the sea. He once said 'The meeting place of land and sea – the coastline – has always been for me the most fascinating area on earth.'

I asked him for his thoughts *About Polzeath*. Here is his salty response:

'From Hartland Point to Padstow Bay is a sailor's grave both night or day' ... so runs the famous ditty, though it puzzles me why the author thereof thought fit to stop at Padstow Bay. There are cliffs and rocks every bit as fiendish and awe-inspiring to a sailor between Padstow and the End of the Land. Maybe the author never strayed so far afield?

I do not blame him (or her) for I was myself captivated on sighting this particular stretch of the Cornish coastline for the first time, having sailed down overnight from Swansea. We anchored in Port Quin Bay just east of Pentire Point by the Mouls islet and it was the start of a life-long love affair.

Since those days I've explored all of the coast on foot, afloat, and in the air. But finally it was this bit in between Port Isaac and Trevose Head enfolding the Camel Estuary that drew me back. Why? Primarily because of the beauty and sheer freedom of it, but also because of the diversity of pleasures it offers.

The Camel river itself, protected as it is by the famous Doom Bar, has become a Mecca for sailing dinghies and all forms of water sports. The Rock Sailing Club offers membership and good facilities for competitive racing as well as other holiday activities. Safe moorings for small shallow-draught craft which may safely take the bottom are available on the Rock side of the river, while Padstow, recently fitted with lock-gates to keep deep water in the inner basin, welcomes the larger boats.

Just outside the Doom Bar is the incomparable Polzeath beach. This is the home of the surfers, and a place to keep well clear of in a boat in all but flat calm conditions. Just opposite, however, a medium-draught craft may find a useful lee under Stepper Point, for the prevailing southwesterly winds skid around the headland to founder on the weather side of Pentire and Polzeath.

Only experienced sailors – no matter what size their craft – are

Looking across to Stepper Point.

advised to venture onto or seaward of the Doom Bar, but that need not preclude enjoyment of the coast from on shore. Both sides of the estuary offer magnificent walks on the coastal footpath, and the sure-of-foot may venture down to innumerable small beaches and coves to explore deep caves at low water. Seals haunt these caves and breed therein at certain times. Swimming is safe provided common sense prevails and one is aware of the state of the tides and tidal streams, which latter may be very strong just after new or full moon.

Port Isaac, an unspoilt fishing harbour, is an invigorating day's walk there and back in the one direction, while Trevone and Mother Ivey's Bay where the lifeboat station is sited makes an invigorating trek, having first crossed the estuary by the passenger ferry (no cars) from Rock.

For the small boat sailor, canoeist, hiker, golfer, and artist, this surfing paradise around Polzeath takes a lot of beating. It is why I have lived here for some forty years!

The roar of the sea, superbly captured by Ray Bishop. He shot this rough sea on Greenaway Rocks between Daymer and Polzeath.

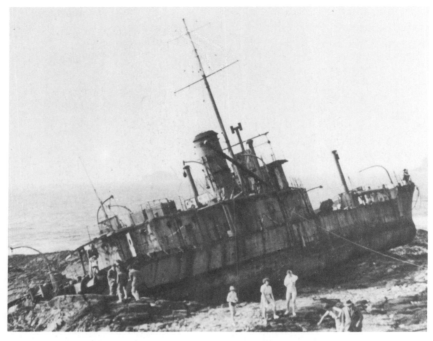

S.S. Medea on the rocks below Greenaway cliffs, Trebetherick, probably 1939. The wreck drew many sightseers.

Cornish Mermaids

MERMAIDS appeared in Cornish legends before the arrival of Christianity. Then they were symbols of Aphrodite, the Goddess of Love. Later, with the coming of the Cornish Mystery plays in the Middle Ages, the Mermaid's role changed to portray the two sides of Christ: half-God and half man just as she is half-woman and half-fish.

There is a mermaid theory surrounding Doom Bar – that menacing sandbank at the mouth of the Camel Estuary. Some say a fisherman shot a mermaid with his arrow and in revenge she cursed Padstow Harbour by placing this sandbar across the entrance.

The same wreck today: photographed on a morning in the autumn of 1992. The seas have left little to recognise after more than 50 years.

Smugglers

TIMES were when this jagged North Cornish coastline of ours was the haunt of smugglers. Writers, particularly writers of fiction, tend to present them in a flattering, romantic light.

In reality many of them were villains: their activities stained with murder and violence, treachery and corruption.

David Mudd, in his excellent *Around and About the Smugglers' Ways,* Bossiney's 200th title, published in 1991, tells of a stranger watching a smuggling operation one dark night:

The truth of what he was seeing struck him.

Going up to one of the men, he asked: 'Where's the magistrate?'

'Havin' dinner with the captain of Dragoons six mile' away'.

'And where's the doctor?'

'Staying home tonight, 'case 'e's needed.'

'Very well then, where's the minister?'

'He's the one holding the lamp'.

It was all supposed to have happened here in North Cornwall but, like Mr Mudd, I'm inclined to think it was born of a 'good story' in a Cornish inn. Either way, it remains an interesting insight into the whole business of smuggling – for smuggling embraced all levels of Cornish society, and in its heyday was a great Cornish industry.

Sabine Baring-Gould, squire and parson for so long at Lewtrenchard just beyond Launceston, and author of that famous hymn *Onward Christian Soldiers*, set his novel *In the Roar of the Sea* here at Polzeath. It is a racy tale of dark nights and darker deeds: a mixture of wrecking and plunder. Its heroine is eighteen-year-old Judith Trevisa who desperately tried to protect her brother from evil influences. She alone dared to defy Captain Coppinger, the man they called Cruel Coppinger. There are many better novels in the Cornish library, but it is a 'good read'. The story of Cruel Coppinger is thought to be based on fact but these unlawful activities probably took place further up the coast.

Parson Hawker of Morwenstow has, in fact, given us an admirable pen portrait of the smuggling operation:

'The rough sea-captain, half smuggler, half pirate, who ran his lugger by beacon-light into some rugged cove among the massive headlands of the shore, and was relieved of his freight by the active and diligent "country-

Sabine Baring-Gould, squire and parson of Lewtrenchard.

side". This was the term allotted to that chosen troop of native sympathis-
ers who were always ready to rescue and conceal the stories that had
escaped the degradation of the gauger's brand. Men yet alive relate with
glee how they used to rush at some well-known signal to the strand, their
small active horses shaved from forelock to tail, smoother than any modern
clip, well soaped or greased from head to foot, so as to slip easily out of any
hostile grasp; and then with a double keg or pack slung on to every nag by
a single girth, away went the whole herd led by some swift well trained
mare, to the inland cave or rocky hold, the shelter of their spoil.'

Mining

THERE was an old miner's saying: 'If you call down any mine in the world, a Cornish voice will call back.' Times were when this had a ring of truth. Ancestors of mine went to America and South Africa. Some Cornishmen took their mining skills overseas; others were starved out of Cornwall through lack of work.

Many visitors, of course, associate mining with inland Cornwall, and it's fair to say places like Redruth and Camborne were the heart of Cornish mining country. But mining also took place at the edge of the ocean.

As you cross Polzeath beach and look around the bay to Pentire Point it is difficult to imagine that lead and silver were mined here for more than two centuries. A.K. Hamilton Jenkin, the Cornish mining historian, records the first mention of the lode in 1580 which he said can still be seen in the cliffs and the Pentire Mine was known to be working in the seventeenth century. In the 1850s under the grand title of the Pentire Glaze and Pentire United Silver-lead Mines, shafts were drained to a depth of two hundred feet by an adit cut from the sea.

But little trace can be seen today of the engine house, steam whim, crusher and water wheel. *The West Briton* records how one Saturday night in 1819 a *'barge conveying lead ore raised from the mine at Pentire Glaze to Padstow, being on her passage from Trebetherick where the ore is shipped, was struck by a heavy sea and being heavily laden, instantly foundered. Of the nine men on board, six perished.'*

A postcard of Polzeath sent in 1904

POLZEATH NORTH CORNWALL. NO 55. J.E.O.

A corner of Polzeath beach: autumn 1992.

Pentire and Rumps Point

WHAT was it Lady Vyvyan, the Cornish writer and traveller, said of the Cornish atmosphere?

'It never beckons you on and on with unfulfilled promise …'

The same is true of certain Cornish places. They have a magnetic quality. Pentire is such a place. To climb the path to Pentire Point is a very worthwhile experience. From the top of this volcanic outcrop a small world of its own spreads out below. You can look back up the estuary and down to Trevose with its lighthouse.

Rumps Point, the eastern flank of Pentire Head looks like a gigantic stegosaurus climbing out of the sea.

The ramparts across this narrow neck of promontory stand out even more when seen silhouetted against the sky from the sea. It's hard to imagine the Iron Age builders of this cliff castle living on this inhospitable headland. Perhaps it was only used for protection when under attack. Yet excavations have shown several huts to have been built within the fortifications and large quantities of animal bones, limpet and mussel shells and pottery indicate considerable occupation. The ramparts were quite sizeable, the middle of the three being built of slate dug from the ditch in front of it and probably topped by a stone parapet and fronted with a revetment of boulders. Large postholes indicate a wooden gate at the entrance through the ramparts. Some wooden fragments were thought to belong to a loom which would certainly lead one to believe that the occupation was more than temporary.

From here you can see Tintagel Castle, on a fine day, Hartland Point and, on rare occasions when the light is just right, Lundy Island, over forty miles away, incredibly seems to rise out of the sea almost within arm's reach.

Arthur Norway maintained this magnificent stretch of cliffs from Pentire was: *'beyond comparison the finest in all Cornwall.'* He said: *'There are deep caves and lofty islands, and changing colours, and beauty in such wild profusion, that the day will surely come when this range of coast will be the most famous in all Cornwall.'*

One day a poet, sitting on the cliffs somewhere here above Polzeath, found the beauty of the coastline stirring thoughts elsewhere. Before long, a poem was beginning to take shape in the man's head. Its opening ran:

*The Rumps, a majestic piece of Cornish coastline caught by the camera of
Ray Bishop, Bossiney's most prolific photographer.*

*With proud thanksgiving, a mother for her children,
England mourns for her dead across the sea ...*

The poet was Laurence Binyon and the poem *For the Fallen*, which,
when published, captured the hearts of the British people, and ensured its
author a kind of immortality. When the 1914-18 war was over, *For the
Fallen* seemed a natural tribute for all who had perished in the conflict, and
was adopted as such by the British Legion. Its famous fourth line – *'They
shall not grow old, as we that are left grow old'* – is even today quoted on
Remembrance Sunday. The poet, that day near Polzeath, was thinking of
the Retreat from Mons.

Port Quin – Poldark and a Puzzle

UP the coast is Port Quin: a beautiful spot, a famous television location – and something of a Cornish puzzle. Port Quin is – or was – all these.

Winston Graham's Poldark novels are among the finest-crafted books about Cornwall, and such is the strong visual quality of Mr Graham's writing they became naturals for the television screen.

When the second *Poldark* series was being shaped, the BBC used a seventeenth century farmhouse and buildings near Port Quin not far from Port Isaac, to represent Nampara.

A working farm, not open to the public, it can be seen distantly from the road leading down to the cove. The narrow inlet of Port Quin was used for location filming, one of the fisherman's cottages representing the home of Captain Blamey. Above the inlet rises Doyden Point, on which stands a Regency Gothic folly, now owned by the National Trust, and familiar to *Poldark* viewers as the home of Dr Dwight Enys. Several scenes were filmed on this headland. More recently, Doyden's 'Castle' – as some call it – was used again on the small screen: this time for Daphne du Maurier's *Jamaica Inn*.

Puzzle? Yes, Port Quin is a Cornish puzzle.

The tiny bay has a fiord-like face, a long finger of water cutting into this dramatic coastline. This, the third valley in St Endellion parish, running down to the Atlantic, was once a busy fishing village. But a story goes that, one night long, long ago, all the men of the village were drowned in a storm at sea – all perishing in the solitary boat owned by the village. The women and the children waited, but nobody returned from that ill-fated fishing trip – and Port Quin became a ghost village.

I say 'a story' because there are different theories about the death of Port Quin. I have come here at evening, when the sun has slowly sunk beyond the rim of the Atlantic, and felt a strange melancholy hanging over the place. Standing on the cliffs as light ebbed from the sky, I remembered too a Canadian who firmly believed he was a son of Port Quin, or, more accurately a descendant, his theory being that, back in the last century, the population of Port Quin emigrated to Canada. A possibility of course.

Did a combination of a poor fishing season and the failure of local

Port Quin: a photograph which captures the mystery and the magic of the place.

mining combine to send the men of Port Quin somewhere else? That's yet another possibility. Or did the men all get cornered by a Press Gang and meet some later even more cruel fate? Other people, though, look for a more materialistic reason: that fishing around the corner at Port Isaac looked a better proposition – and the villagers simply left.

The Folly at Doyden, Port Quin.

Winwaloe, Polzeath, the house where the Roman Catholic Archbishop Cardinal Bernard Griffin died suddenly while on holiday in 1956. This photograph was taken within twenty-four hours of the Archbishop's death. In the background is Pentire Head.

The Weather – and the Coastal Path

THE weather is a regular – some would say overworked – ploy in British conversation. I am a collector of old Cornish picture post cards, and many of the cards are preoccupied with 'the weather'. Often those from North Cornwall mention 'very windy'. One wonders whether those Victorian and Edwardian visitors realized they were coming to face the Atlantic Ocean.

North Cornwall, like all Cornwall, cannot boast a settled climate, but we do get some beautiful days and the fact our tourist season has stretched in the last quarter of a century is partly confirmation of the fine weather we often get in spring and autumn. The bonus of early and late holidays for visitors is that they then avoid congestion on both beaches and roads. I am writing these words on the 30th day of December and we have just had a string of brilliantly sunlit days: perfect for walks along the North Cornish coast.

And don't be deterred by what we call 'bad weather', days when the painter J.M.W. Turner, who came to North Cornwall, would have produced some of his most atmospheric pictures. The Atlantic on a stormy day can be

Cattle grazing: old Polzeath from Tinner's Hill.

Surfing at Polzeath: good off-shore winds.

a thrilling sight, and a misty morning can add its own peculiar magic.

Our cliff walks are, of course, some of the greatest free pleasures in the British Isles, and some of the walks hereabouts are among the finest in the whole of the UK.

It was in 1973 that Lord Caradon formally opened the 272 mile long Cornish Coastal Path: the result of many years' work between the County

Council and the Footpaths Preservation Society which meant obtaining permission from landowners and linking new stretches to existing paths. I must stress though that when you cross a field you are walking through a farmer's workshop. Indeed, grass is an important crop for the farmer. So please stick to footpaths, respect private property – and resist the temptation to wander – or even trespass.

The wild life of Cornwall is best seen in the landscape and not when we uproot it and put in into a vase or glass pot. By picking flowers, carving on trees and rocks, or disturbing wild animals and birds, we not only destroy a bit of Cornwall but we also spoil other people's pleasure.

Walks along these cliff paths do two things. They provide us with many beautiful *and* unforgettable views and they can be energising: a tonic in fact.

It was a wise Greek who recalled 'I wanted to know, so I went to see.' I advise you to do just that about Polzeath.

Chapel Hill in 1920: a narrower road than we know today – and quieter too. Little then to disturb these neighbours chatting as they go about their chores on a bright summer's day.

Acknowledgements

I wish to thank the Stott family of Polzeath for commissioning this publication. Their shop, near the beach at Polzeath, has been a loyal supporter of Bossiney publishing over the years.

I am also indebted to Brenda Duxbury, my co-author of The River Camel. *That now out of print Bossiney title has provided valuable background material. Once more thanks to the Cornish Studies Library at Redruth, and Terry Knight in particular, Angela Larcombe for her thoughtful editing, the various photographers, Maggie Ginger for her cover design and Sally Dodd for turning my untidy typing into an impeccable manuscript.*

Last but not least I owe a special debt to Mr and Mrs Ralph Tellam-Hocking who know this corner of North Cornwall so well and love it dearly – they have read the manuscript and lent some splendid old photographs.

MORE BOSSINEY BOOKS ...

CURIOUS CORNWALL
by Michael Williams
Words and pictures prove Cornwall has more than her share of things curious.
'... what insights, words of wisdom about Cornwall and the Cornish experience ... not in any forced manner or through any artificial device of compression. I suppose it all arises from a life of interest in and experience of the Cornish scene.'   Dr James Whetter, **The Cornish Banner**

STRANGE STORIES OF CORNWALL
Six writers prove that fact is often stranger than fiction.
'Thought-provoking ... little-known odd occurrences, strange places and eccentric characters.'   Adrian Ruck, **Cornish & Devon Post**

THE CRUEL CORNISH SEA
by David Mudd
David Mudd selects more than 30 Cornish shipwrecks, spanning 400 years, in his fascinating account of seas and a coastline that each year claim their toll of human lives.
'This is an important book.'   Lord St Levan, **The Cornish Times**

DAPHNE du MAURIER COUNTRY
by Martyn Shallcross
A special look at Cornwall in which the internationally-famous novelist set important stories.
'A treasure chest for those who love Cornwall and the du Maurier novels.'
Valerie Mitchell,   **The Packet Group of Newspapers**

OLD PICTURE POSTCARDS OF CORNWALL
by Sara Paston-Williams

GHOSTS OF CORNWALL
by Peter Underwood
Peter Underwood, President of the Ghost Club, journeys across haunted Cornwall. Photographs of haunted sites and drawings of ghostly characters all combine to prove that Cornwall is indeed a mystic land.

PARANORMAL IN THE WESTCOUNTRY
by Michael Williams

MORE BOSSINEY BOOKS ...

MYSTERIES IN THE CORNISH LANDSCAPE
by Tamsin Thomas

DISCOVERING BODMIN MOOR
by E.V. Thompson

LEGENDS OF CORNWALL
by Sally Jones

SUPERNATURAL INVESTIGATION
by Michael Williams

Investigations into a whole range of Supernatural subjects: ghosts and ghostly music, dreams and time slips, superstition and theatre ghosts.

MYSTERIES OF THE SOUTH WEST
by Tamsin Thomas of BBC Radio Cornwall

'Complete with dozens of photographs and drawings, Tamsin Thomas presents a fascinating word-picture tour.'   **North Cornwall Advertiser**

NORTH CORNWALL REFLECTIONS
by Hilda Hambly

KING ARTHUR IN THE WEST
by Felicity Young and Michael Williams

BODMIN MOOR THROUGH THE YEARS
by E.V. Thompson

GHOSTLY ENCOUNTERS
by Peter Underwood

We shall be pleased to send you our catalogue giving full details of our growing list of titles for Devon, Cornwall, Dorset and Somerset as well as forthcoming publications. If you have difficulty in obtaining our titles, write direct to Bossiney Books, Land's End, St Teath, Bodmin, Cornwall.

Back cover: a photograph by Ray Bishop of Wadebridge showing tamarisk trees at Daymer with Stepper Point away on the left.